EVERYDAY
IMMORTALITY

EVERYDAY IMMORTALITY

A Concise Course in
Spiritual Transformation

DEEPAK CHOPRA

GRAMERCY BOOKS
NEW YORK

This 2003 edition published by Gramercy Books, an imprint of
Random House Value Publishing, a division of Random House, Inc.,
New York by arrangements with Harmony Books, New York.

Gramercy is a registered trademark and the colophon is a trademark
of Random House, Inc.

Harmony Books is a registered trademark and the colophon is a
trademark of Random House, Inc.

Printed in the United States of America

Designed by Leonard Henderson

Random House
New York • Toronto • London • Sydney • Auckland
www.randomhouse.com

A catalog record for this title is available from the Library of Congress

ISBN: 0-517-22248-5

9 8 7 6 5 4 3 2 1

Acknowledgments

$\mathcal{S}$OME OF THE SENTENCES IN THIS BOOK ARE DIRECT TRANS-lations of commonly used expressions in Vedantic teachings. My personal debt of gratitude goes to all the great luminaries of Vedanta, but especially to the teachings of Patanjali, Shankara, Ramakrishna, Vivekananda, Yogananda, Ramana Maharshi, Sri Aurobindo, Krishnamurti, Maharishi Mahesh Yogi, Nisar-gadatta Maharaj, and also to the great Western Rishis, including Einstein, Bohr, Heisenberg, John Bell, David Bohm, Eugene Wigner, Fred Alan Wolf, and many others.

Many thanks to my colleagues and staff at the Chopra Center for Well Being and Infinite Possibilities. Thank you— David Simon, Roger Gabriel, Carolyn Rangel, Jennie Pugh, Veronique Franceus, Gayle Rose, Nan Johnson, Barbara Dono-hue, Muriel Nellis, Arielle Ford, Renee Dunn, and most espe-cially my family for your loving support.

Thanks also to my friends at Harmony Books, especially Chip Gibson, Steve Magnuson, Patricia Gift, Tina Constable, and Peter Guzzardi.

Introduction

*F*OR THOUSANDS OF YEARS HUMAN BEINGS HAVE ASKED the question "Who am I?" Aside from great spiritual masters the vast majority of humans have no knowledge of their true identity as spiritual beings with unbounded potential. As a result the history of so-called civilized man has been one of conflict and destruction.

Today the discoveries of modern science are giving us new insights into our true nature. We are on the threshold of a new era, and we stand equipped with a new kind of knowledge, a knowledge that could either be our savior or our destroyer. We have the choice to either jump into the abyss of illusion and igno-rance or soar into the experience of reality and enlightenment. But to experience the new reality we must first encounter the death of our old identity as skin-encapsulated egos enmeshed in a bag of flesh and bones, confined to a prison of space, time, and causation, squeezed into the volume of a body and the span of a lifetime. We must escape the prison of the known and soar joyfully into the unknown. As the great Sufi poet Rumi said, "When I die I shall soar with angels and when I die to the angels what I shall become you cannot imagine."

What imprisons us in our old identity is an old kind of logic, a logic founded on the superstition of materialism. The new logic based on the insights of quantum physics and the experience of meditation liberates us to a new experience of ourselves. Elsewhere in my books and tapes I have dealt extensively with the concept of the quantum mechanical body, so I am not going to go into a theoretical discussion of this here. (For those interested in an in-depth discussion and theory of the quantum mechanical body, my book and tape series titled *Quantum Healing* is a good reference guide.)

In the following pages I want to give you an appreciation of the quantum mechanical body and of quantum reality so that you can actually experience what seers have called higher states of consciousness. In these higher states of consciousness, the highest of which is referred to as unity consciousness, conflicts resolve and one experiences a reverence and love for all life in the universe. As you go through the pages of this book you will find a series of sentences that will serve as primary statements or insights. Each statement also may be regarded as a sutra or a koan.

For best results I suggest that you read one sentence at a time and ponder the meaning of that one sentence. Sometimes it will be very obvious, and you will get immediate insight into the meaning of the koan. In some cases the insight will not be so immediate, and you may have to spend a number of hours or days or weeks with a particular sutra or statement. But ultimately, as you continue to ponder the meaning of the sentence and pay attention to it, a flash of insight will come into your awareness. As a result of that flash of insight, your awareness and your experience of yourself and of the world will begin to change, and you will begin to slowly experience a state of joyful carefreeness and love that will stay with you more and more.

These exercises should be performed at your own pace. Each sentence must be fully understood and comprehended and give you a new insight before you move on to the next. As you progress through these exercises, understanding and insight unfold in sequence. Before you read a sentence it is best to sit down and take some time to relax either through meditation or through silently watching your breath, which could take about five to ten minutes. After reading a new page, sit silently for another five to ten minutes and ponder the meaning of that particular sentence. If the meaning and the insight are immediately obvious, you should move to the next sentence. Otherwise keep that sentence alive in your awareness for an extended period of time, coming back to it again and again, keeping your attention on it and examining it until the meaning is clear or until a flash of insight comes to you. If you do this on a daily basis, taking one sentence a day, or moving at whatever pace suits you, the knowledge in these pages will progressively unfold. Metabolized in this regular, incremental way, the knowledge will automatically lead to a shift in consciousness.

These exercises are the modern version of Gyana Yoga, which is the yoga of knowledge. A sutra is a statement that can cause a shift in consciousness. Sometimes it may appear to be full of contradictions, and perhaps seem irrational. Yet at the same time it can provide a better framework for understanding the nature of our physical world, and our true nature. If some of these statements seem contrary to common sense, this is because they are coming into conflict with your everyday experience of the world through your senses. This is the world you experience in the ordinary waking state of consciousness. But once understood and incorporated into your awareness, the sutras can lead to new insights that open the gateway to higher states of consciousness. Gyana Yoga, the yoga of knowledge, has often been considered the most difficult but also the most gratifying road to enlightenment. By walking the path laid out in the pages ahead, we can gain a glimpse of this higher state of reality. So let's begin.

EVERYDAY
IMMORTALITY

*T*he material universe and the physical

body that I experience through my senses

are only one aspect of reality.

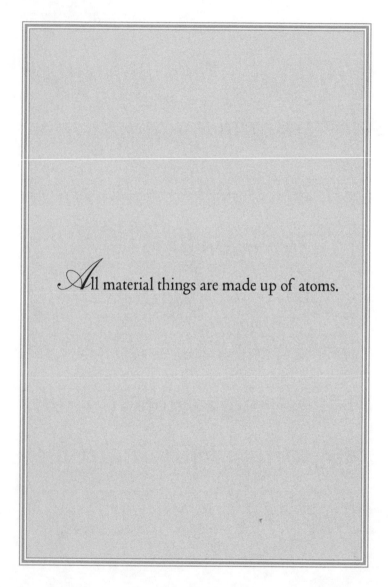

*A*ll material things are made up of atoms.

*A*toms are composed of subatomic

particles moving at lightning speeds

through huge empty spaces.

$\mathcal{S}$ubatomic particles are not material

things; they are fluctuations of energy

and information in a huge void.

$\mathcal{S}$ubatomic particles flicker in and out of

existence depending on whether I am

watching them or not.

$\mathscr{B}$efore my decision to observe them,

subatomic particles are probability

amplitudes or mathematical ghosts

in a field of infinite possibilities.

When I make the choice to observe the subatomic world of mathematical ghosts, the ghosts freeze into space-time events or particles that ultimately manifest as matter.

My physical body and the body of the

physical universe are both proportionately

as void as intergalactic space.

The essential nature of my material body

and that of the solid-appearing universe

is that they are both nonmaterial.

They are made up of non-stuff.

*M*y material body and the body of the

Universe both flicker in and out of existence

at the speed of light.

$\mathcal{M}$y nervous system cannot process these quantum events at the speed at which they are really happening, so it decodes the energy and information soup of the Universe into the experience of solid three-dimensional material bodies.

When I decide to observe the quantum

soup of the Universe, made up of non-stuff,

it manifests in my awareness as a physical

body that I experience as mine, and other

bodies that I experience as the Universe.

*I*n my decision to become an observer,

I create the experience of my physical body

and also that of the physical Universe.

$\mathcal{M}$y brain is made up of the same non-stuff or void that exists everywhere. It is a decoding instrument that moves through a vibrating dance of energy and information, and, as a result of this interaction, I start to experience material and solid things.

*M*y brain is a sensor that tunes in to a

nonlocal, omnipresent vibrating field

of infinite frequencies.

*M*y body is an experience that I have

in space and time. It has a location in space,

and it exists in time. It has a beginning,

a middle, and an ending.

$\mathcal{M}$y world is a continuum of
experiences and is therefore comprised
of space-time events. It exists as objects
in space that have beginnings, middles,
and endings.

My brain is an instrument that I use

to have experiences.

*W*here is the me that is using this instrument (called the brain) to have these experiences called the body, which gets born, moves through space and time, and then dies?

*M*e is the experiencer behind every

experience, the thinker behind every thought,

the seer behind every scenery, the observer

behind every observation.

$\mathcal{T}$he experience changes, but the experiencer remains the same. The thought comes and goes, the thinker is always there; the scenery transforms, but the seer remains unchanged, eternal. The real me is the seer, not the scenery.

I cannot experience the experiencer by using my senses, because when I use my senses I begin to have experiences, and then I am no longer with myself, I am with my experience.

I cannot experience the experiencer

by thinking thoughts because when I am

thinking thoughts I can no longer be

with myself, the thinker.

*T*houghts are experiences. The thinker

is the experiencer. Perhaps the thought is the

thinker in disguise, and the experience

is the experiencer in disguise.

*T*his is the dilemma.

Is the thinker the thought?

Is the experiencer the experience?

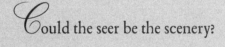

Could the seer be the scenery?

Could the thinker be the thought?

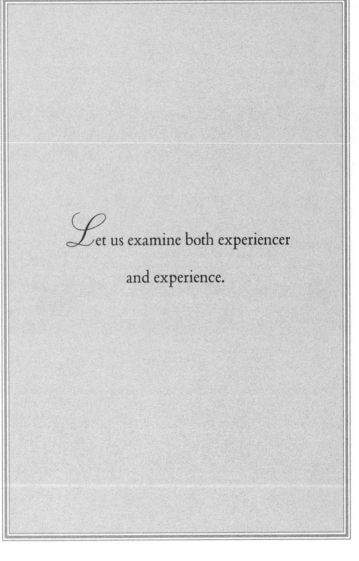

*L*et us examine both experiencer

and experience.

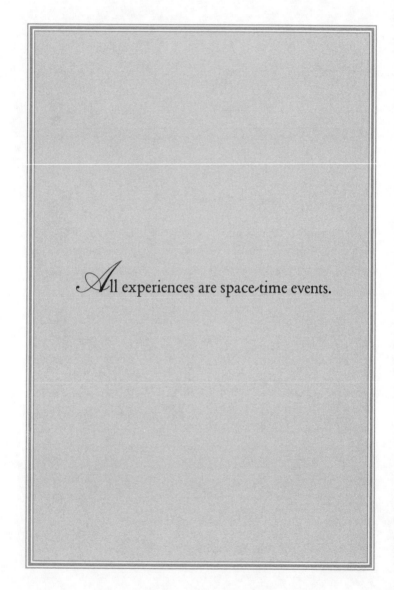

All experiences are space-time events.

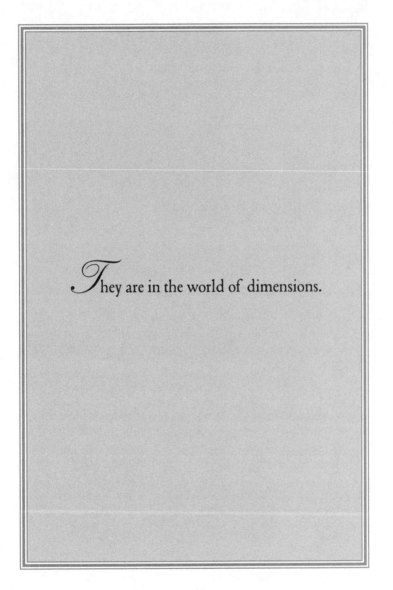

They are in the world of dimensions.

*M*y body occupies space.

It has height, width, volume.

It exists in time.

It is time bound.

Even thoughts are flickering space-time events. They occur for a flicker of an instant and have a beginning, a middle, and an end. For a flicker of an instant, they occupy a space and a location in awareness.

$\mathcal{T}$herefore all experience is time bound.

The experiencer, on the other hand,

being the silent, nonchanging witness

in every experience, is timeless.

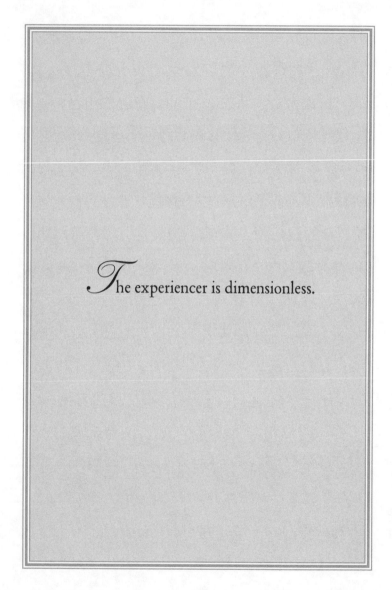

The experiencer is dimensionless.

The experiencer occupies no space.

$\mathcal{S}$ince the experiencer is there before the

experience and is there after the experience,

it is always there, and being always there,

it is eternal.

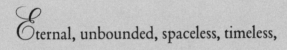

Eternal, unbounded, spaceless, timeless,

dimensionless, the experiencer is Spirit.

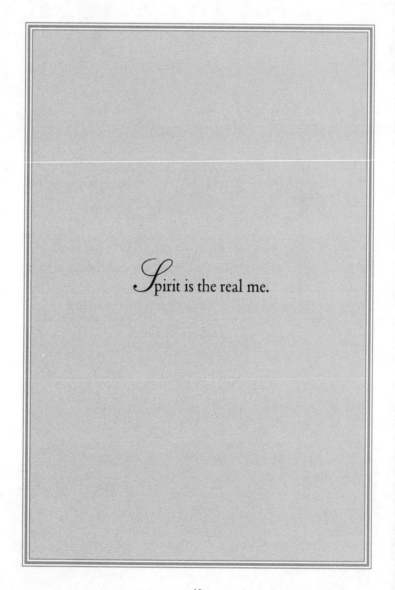

Spirit is the real me.

*N*onmaterial and dimensionless,

Spirit can neither be created nor destroyed.

*S*pirit is spaceless, timeless,

and dimensionless.

*F*ire cannot burn it and water cannot wet it,

wind cannot dry it, weapons cannot kill it,

eternal and unbounded and nonchanging,

without beginning and without ending;

it is nowhere in particular and

everywhere in general.

*T*his spirit is the essential me.

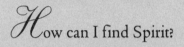How can I find Spirit?

Not by thinking.

Not by doing.

Only by Being.

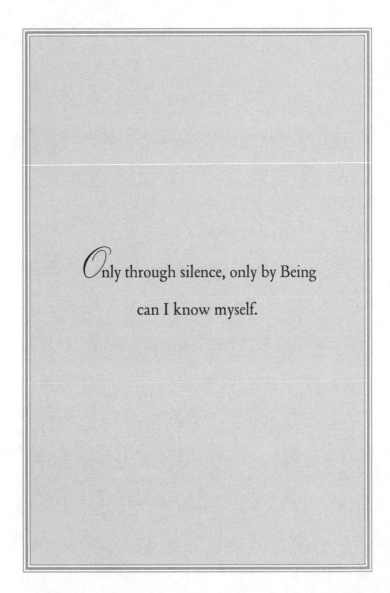

$\mathcal{O}$nly through silence, only by Being

can I know myself.

When I am not using memories, when I am not anticipating, when I am just being, then I am just awareness. Then I experience myself as the timeless factor in the midst of time-bound experience.

As Spirit I know that my persona

changes, I don't.

I look into the mirror, and I see the

change in my persona from ten years ago.

But the *me* that is looking is unchanged.

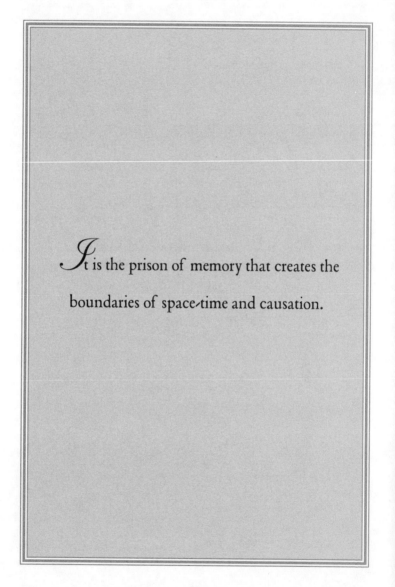

$\mathcal{I}$t is the prison of memory that creates the

boundaries of space-time and causation.

When I escape the prison of memory,

I experience the boundless in the

midst of boundaries.

*M*emories are frozen pictures of

space-time events.

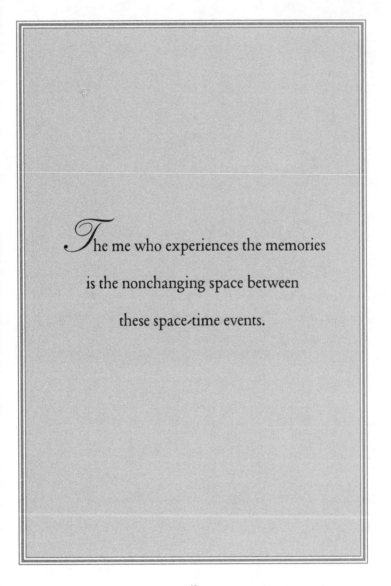

$\mathcal{T}$he me who experiences the memories

is the nonchanging space between

these space⁄time events.

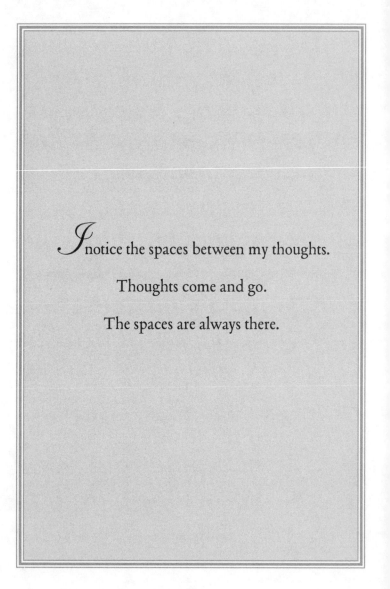

$\mathcal{I}$notice the spaces between my thoughts.

Thoughts come and go.

The spaces are always there.

I am now noticing the spaces between written words, spaces between objects, spaces between thoughts, spaces between sounds, spaces between musical notes, spaces inside a cup, around it, and outside it. I am noticing spaces, spaces everywhere. They are all the same spaces, and they are always there. Before the thoughts came, after they left, the space is. Before the music was born and after it died— the space is. Before the words were uttered and after the speech was silent—the space is. Before and after death—the space is.

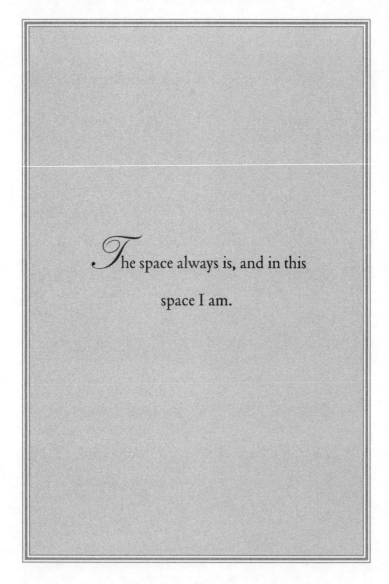

The space always is, and in this

space I am.

Before birth I am.

After death I am.

I always am.

*W*hen I quantify space I create time.

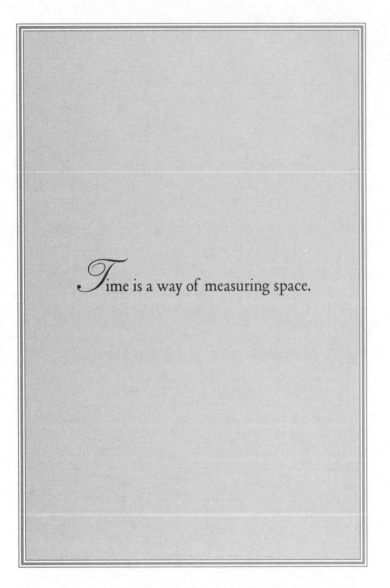

Time is a way of measuring space.

When I quantify time I create space.

Space is a way of measuring time.

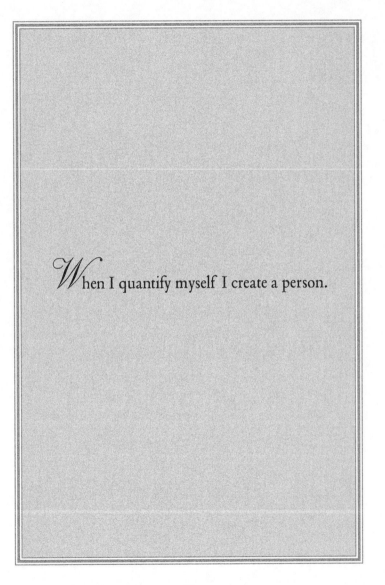

When I quantify myself I create a person.

When I notice the spaces between sounds

and the spaces between words and also

the spaces between my thoughts and the

background silence behind everything,

I realize that all these spaces

are the same space.

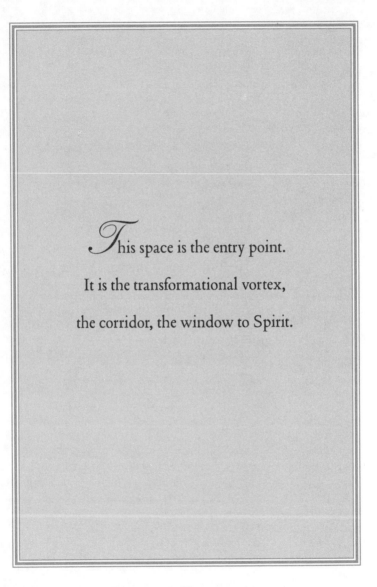

$\mathcal{T}$his space is the entry point.

It is the transformational vortex,

the corridor, the window to Spirit.

*S*pirit is beyond the void of space.

This realm, beyond the void,

is not an empty nothingness;

it is the womb of creation.

*N*ature goes to the same place to create

a galaxy of stars, a cluster of nebulas,

a rain forest, a human body, or a thought.

That place is Spirit.

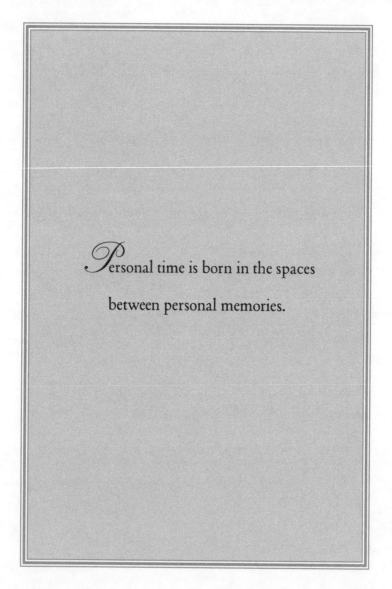

Personal time is born in the spaces

between personal memories.

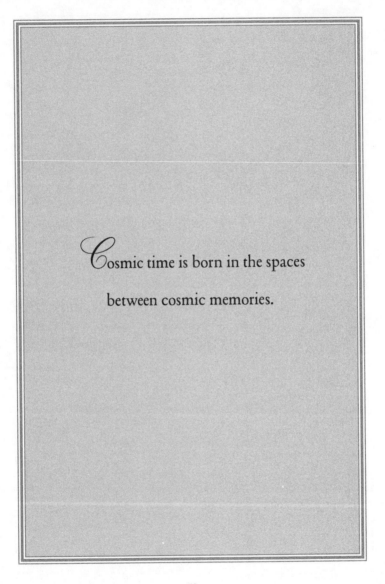

Cosmic time is born in the spaces

between cosmic memories.

$\mathcal{S}$pirit is the potentiality for

space-time events.

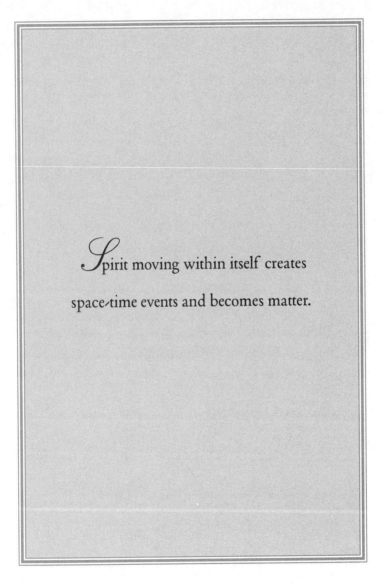

$\mathcal{S}$pirit moving within itself creates

space-time events and becomes matter.

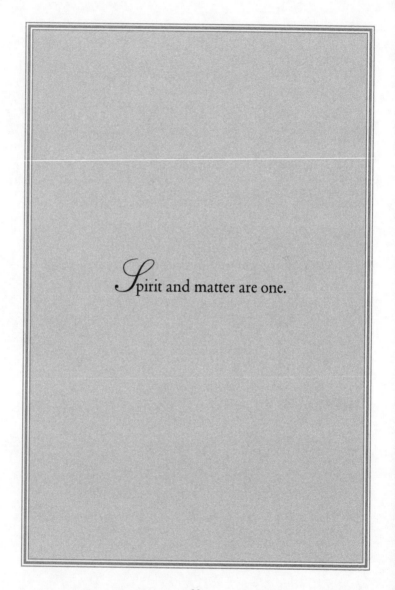

Spirit and matter are one.

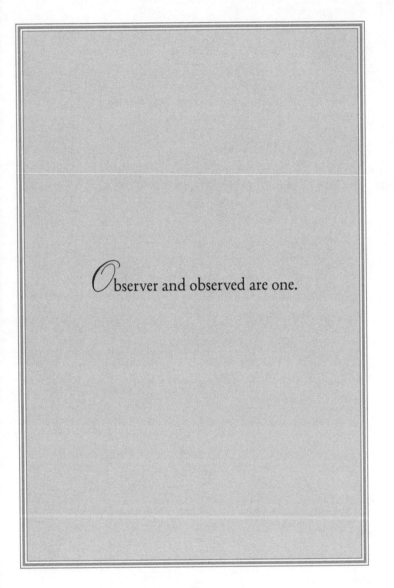

Observer and observed are one.

*S*eer and scenery are one.

The seer, the observer, the experiencer,

the thinker, the field, and pure awareness

are all different words to describe Spirit.

Spirit (the observer) has no height, no width, no length, no breadth, no volume, no space, no duration. It is eternal, bounded, ineffable, and abstract.

*S*pirit is invisible. It is soundless. It is

without texture, without taste, without smell.

It is dimensionless, spaceless, and timeless.

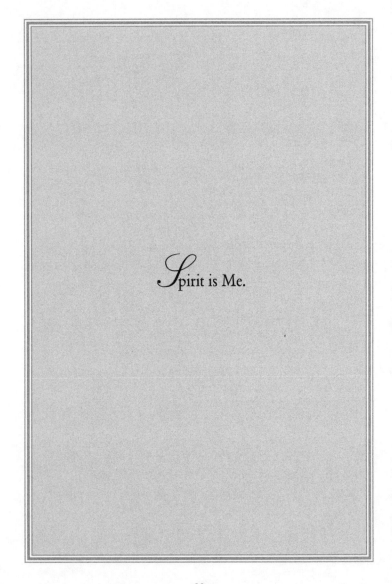

*S*pirit is Me.

Spirit is the immeasurable potential of all

that was, is, and will be, and it is Me.

It is the Field.

When the Field vibrates it creates waves.

The vibrating Field—with its waves

of intelligence, information, and energy—

is the invisible source of the fabric

of the space-time continuum.

*W*aves of intelligence are vibrations

of Spirit.

*W*aves of intelligence are also my thoughts

and all thoughts everywhere.

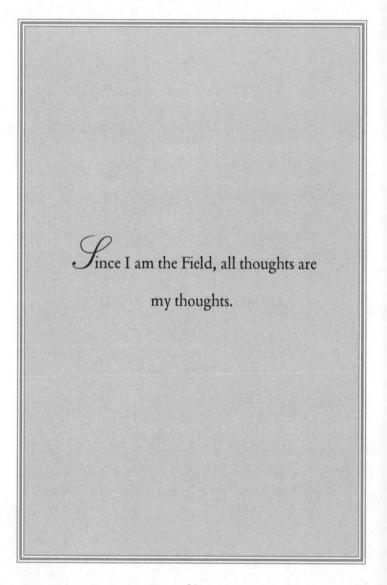

$\mathcal{S}$ince I am the Field, all thoughts are

my thoughts.

*S*ome thoughts are experienced

more personally.

I call them mine.

*S*ome thoughts I experience less personally.

I call these other people's thoughts and also

the thoughts of animals and Nature.

*S*ome thoughts I experience inside my personal body, and some I experience outside my body. Some are personal, others are impersonal; however, all thoughts are equally mine.

*V*ibrations in the Field are thoughts in
consciousness. They are quantum events
in the space-time continuum. These are
the ways the observer becomes the process
of observation and the experiencer
becomes the process of experience.
This is the mind in action.

*W*hen these vibrations condense or freeze,

matter is born.

$\mathcal{F}$rozen vibrations are matter.

$\mathcal{F}$rozen vibrations are the birth of matter.

They are the birth of the web of space-time

events. These are the *things* that occupy space

and have duration in time.

*M*atter is the birth of particles

from waves.

*A*ll particles are frozen waves.

*A*ll material bodies are condensations

of frozen vibrations.

*M*atter is the world of material objects.

It is the scenery, the object of experience,

the observed.

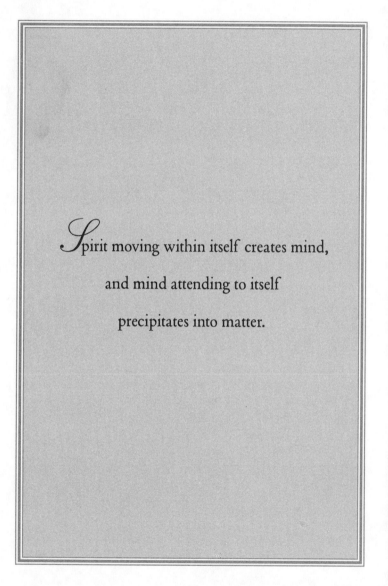

*S*pirit moving within itself creates mind,

and mind attending to itself

precipitates into matter.

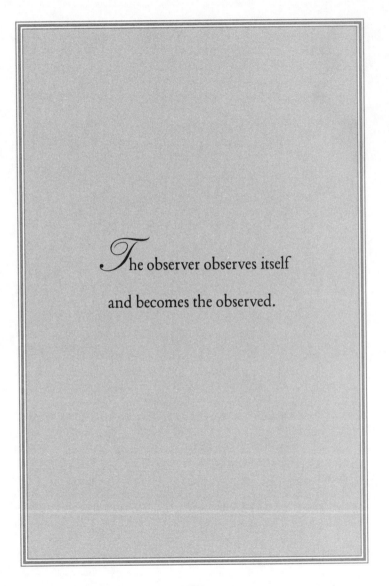

The observer observes itself

and becomes the observed.

*T*he seer sees itself

and becomes the scenery.

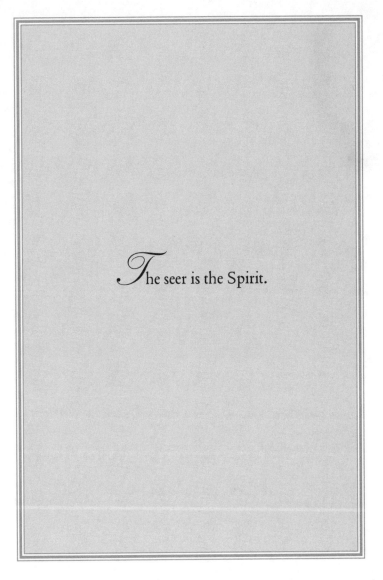

The seer is the Spirit.

The seeing is the mind.

The scenery is the world.

Seer, scenery, and seeing are One.

Spirit, mind, and matter are One.

Creation is the self interacting with itself

and experiencing itself. Sometimes it

is the seer, sometimes it is the seeing,

sometimes it is the scenery.

*A*ll that exists is me interacting with

myself and experiencing myself as Spirit,

mind, and matter.

I experience myself subjectively
as the mind and objectively as the body
and the world.

*T*he body, mind, and world are just

different manifestations of myself as

different forms and phenomena.

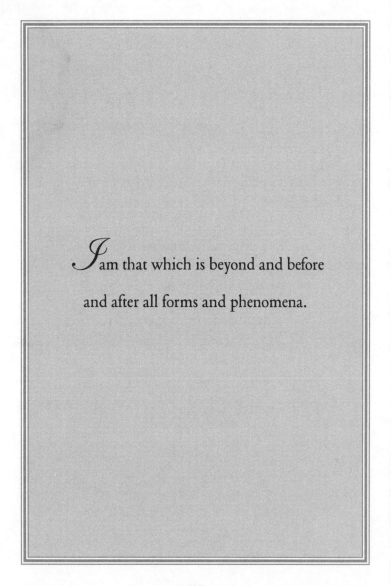

$\mathcal{I}$ am that which is beyond and before

and after all forms and phenomena.

am that.

You are that.

That alone is.

*P*hysicists describe four forces of nature. These are the strong interaction, the weak interaction, electromagnetism, and gravity.

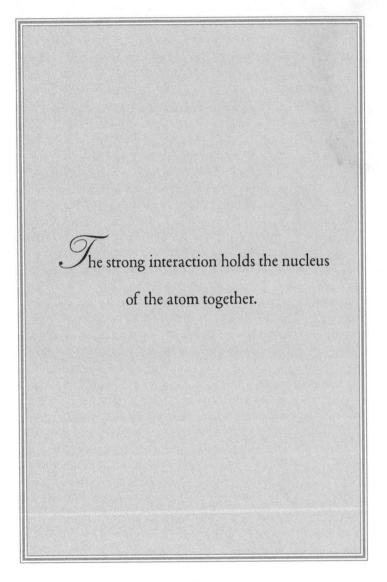

The strong interaction holds the nucleus

of the atom together.

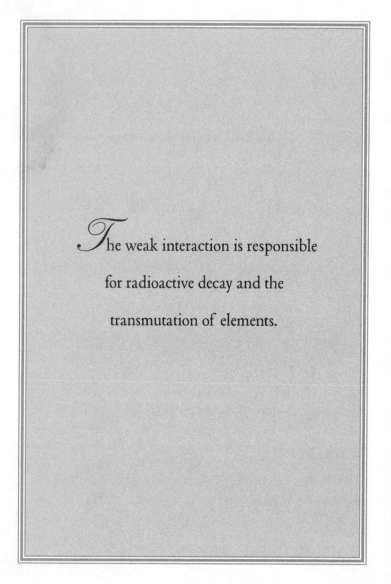

The weak interaction is responsible

for radioactive decay and the

transmutation of elements.

Electromagnetism gives rise to heat,

light, electricity, and magnetism.

*G*ravity holds the planets together

and makes the world go around.

These four forces (electromagnetism, gravity, strong and weak interactions) are the matrix of the material universe.

The four fundamental forces of Nature

come from one Unified Field. The Unified

Field is the source of creation—the dancer.

*T*he Unified Field is the field

of dimensionless reality. It is the

potentiality for all the information energy

and matter in the Universe.

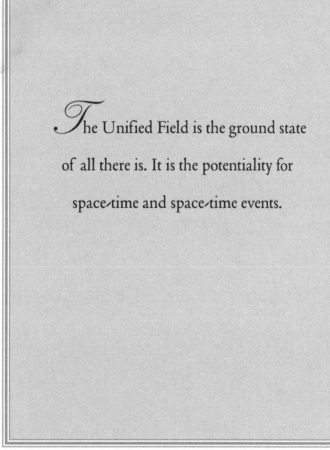

$\mathcal{T}$he Unified Field is the ground state

of all there is. It is the potentiality for

space-time and space-time events.

The curvature of space-time

is called gravity.

It is part of the dance,

the process of creation.

The friction within space-time is electromagnetism, which is heat, light, electricity, and energy. It is also part of the dance—the process of creation.

$\mathcal{T}$he condensation of space-time as weak

and strong forces creates matter—the earth,

water, fire, air, and space. It is the expression

of the dance or that which is created.

Earth, fire, water, air, and space are matter

in its solid, metabolic, liquid, gaseous,

and quantum mechanical forms.

*S*ince the Unified Field is the ground state

of everything and since the Spirit is also the

ground state of everything, the Spirit and

Unified Field are One.

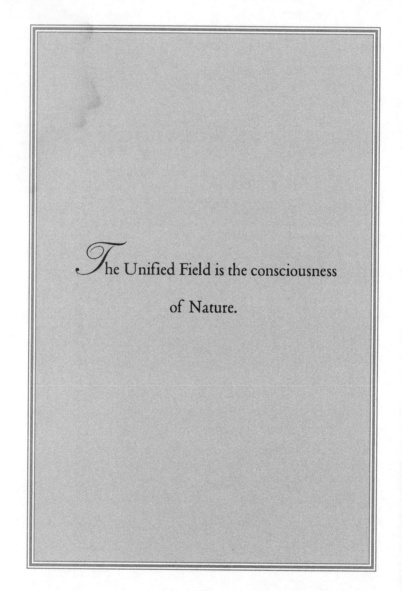

$\mathcal{T}$he Unified Field is the consciousness

of Nature.

The forces of Nature—heat, light, electricity, magnetism, strong and weak forces, and gravity—are *the mind of Nature.*

*T*he material universe is the body

of Nature.

Since I and the Unified Field are One in

our ground state, I am the witness in the

Unified Field, my thoughts or mind are just

a different manifestation of the same forces

of Nature that we call heat, light, electricity,

magnetism, and gravity. My body is just a

different manifestation of the same body

that I call the Universe.

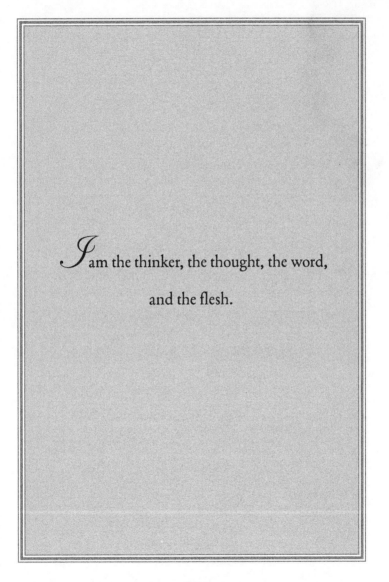

I am the thinker, the thought, the word,

and the flesh.

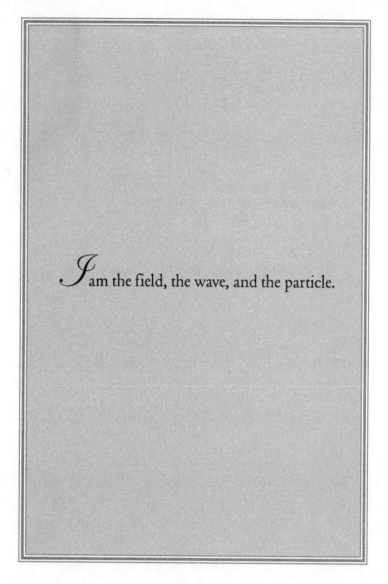

I am the field, the wave, and the particle.

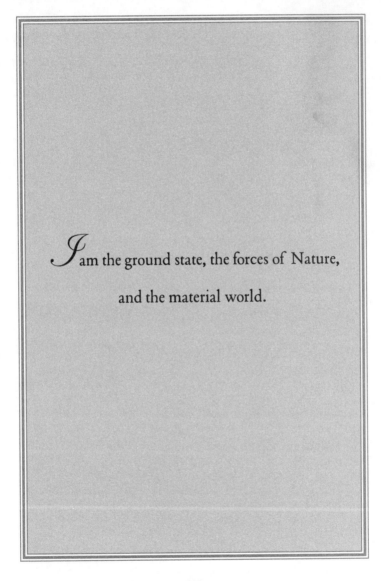

I am the ground state, the forces of Nature,

and the material world.

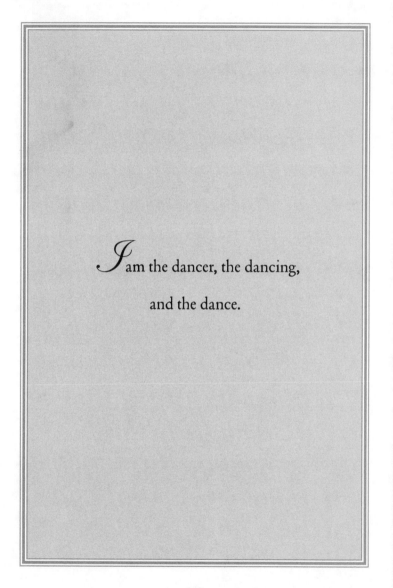

I am the dancer, the dancing,

and the dance.

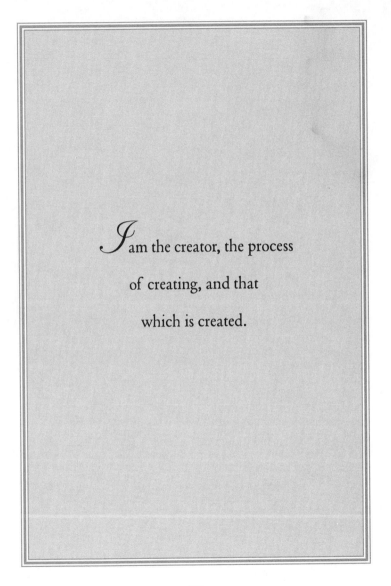

$\mathcal{I}$am the creator, the process

of creating, and that

which is created.

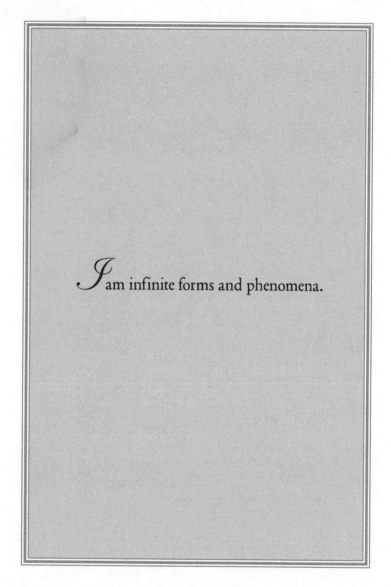

I am infinite forms and phenomena.

I have invented space.

I have created time.

*I*manifest as gravity, which holds the planets and makes the world go around.

I am the source of all energy

and all its forms.

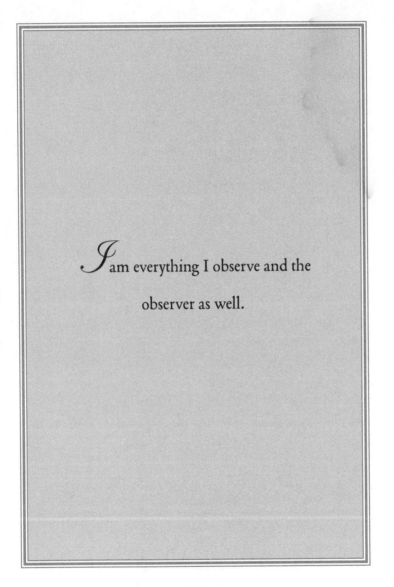

I am everything I observe and the

observer as well.

I am Existence.

As Existence I am before the beginning, during the middle, and after the end of all forms and phenomena. I am the chair I sit on and the clothes I am wearing and the mountains that I see and the stars and distant galaxies. I am everything in general and anything in particular.

When I see light and color,

I am light and color.

*W*hen I hear sound and music,

I am sound and music.

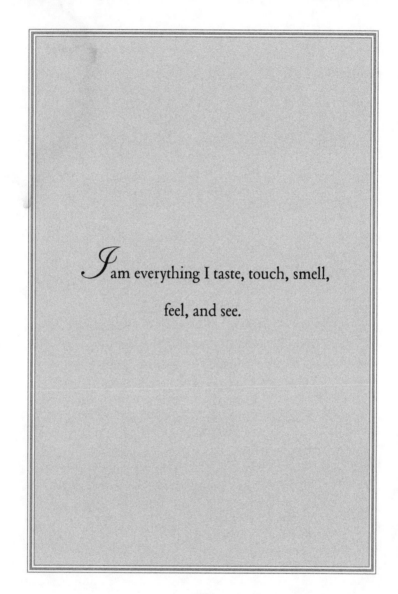

I am everything I taste, touch, smell,

feel, and see.

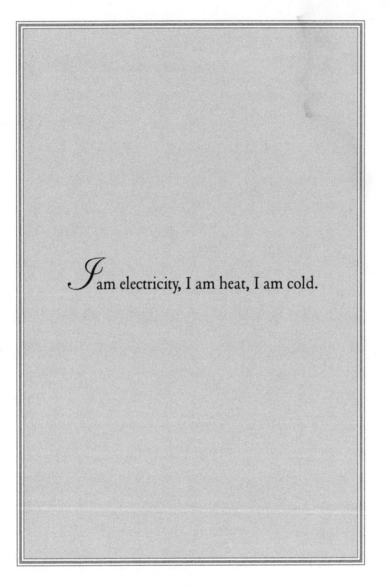

$\mathcal{I}$am electricity, I am heat, I am cold.

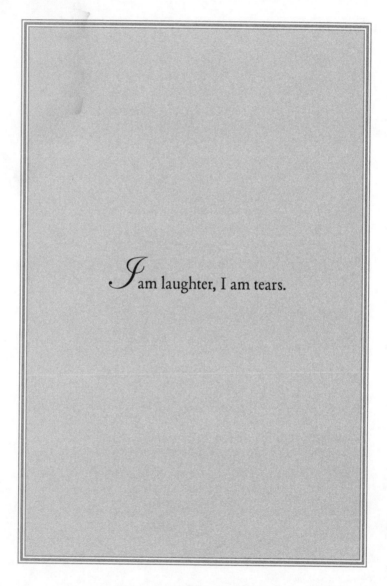

$\mathcal{I}$am laughter, I am tears.

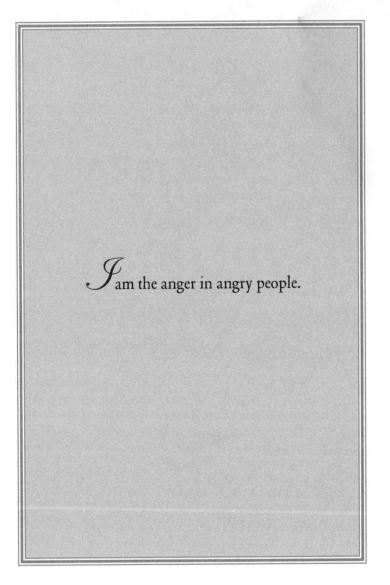

$\mathcal{I}$am the anger in angry people.

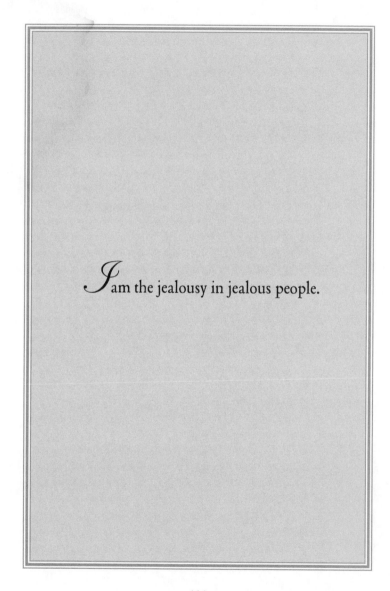

$\mathcal{I}$am the jealousy in jealous people.

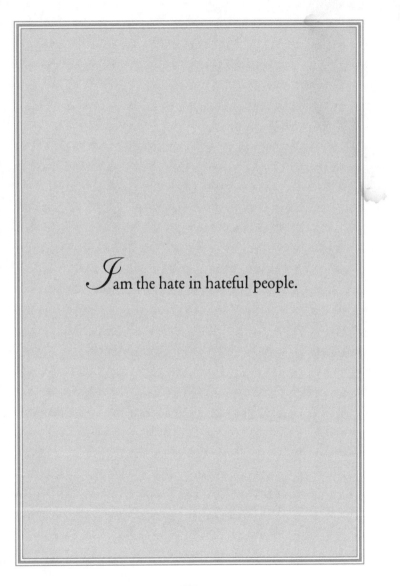

*I*am the hate in hateful people.

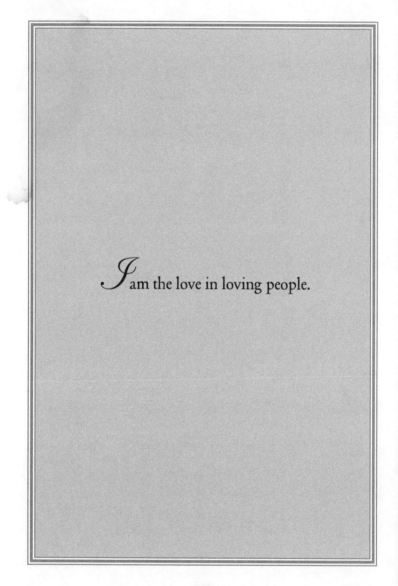

$\mathcal{I}$am the love in loving people.

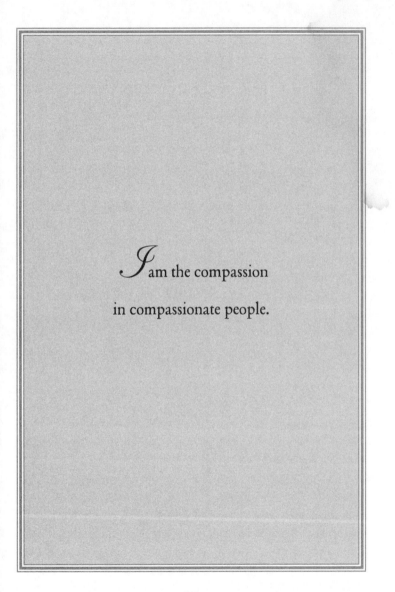

$\mathcal{I}$am the compassion

in compassionate people.

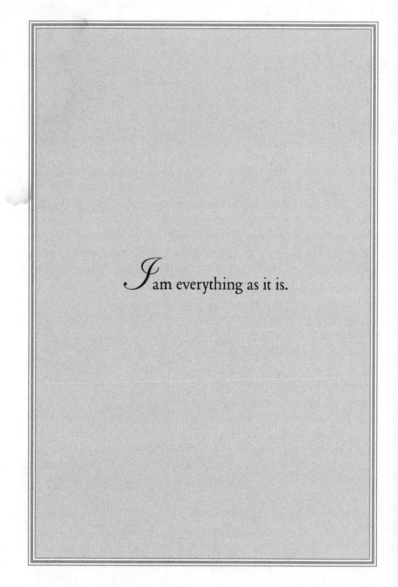

$\mathcal{I}$am everything as it is.

I have no need to attack myself

or anybody.

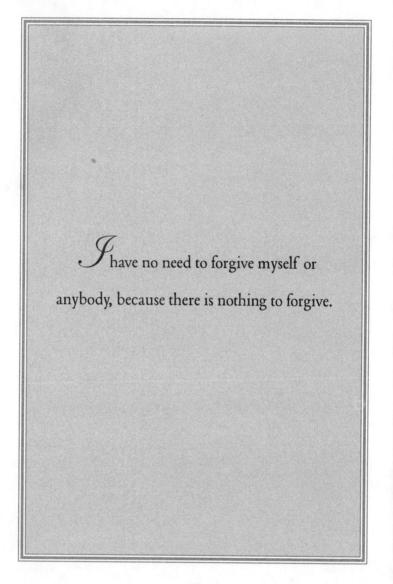

$\mathcal{I}$ have no need to forgive myself or

anybody, because there is nothing to forgive.

I have no need to defend myself

or anybody.

I have no need to hurt myself

or anybody.

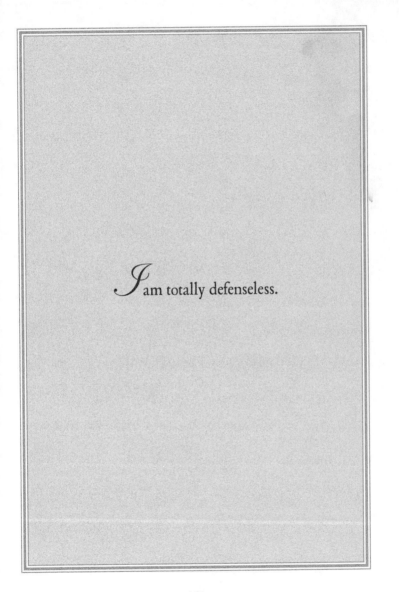

$\mathcal{I}$am totally defenseless.

*I*n my total defenselessness is my

invincibility.

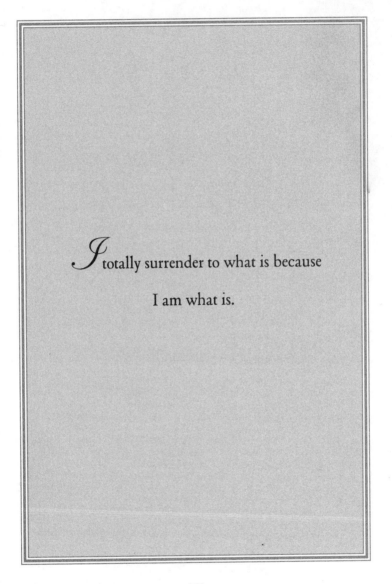

I totally surrender to what is because

I am what is.

In my world, I am whatever is. There is nothing to forget, nothing to forgive, nothing to remember, no grudges to hold, no conflicts to fight, no one to spite; even in conflict there is no conflict.

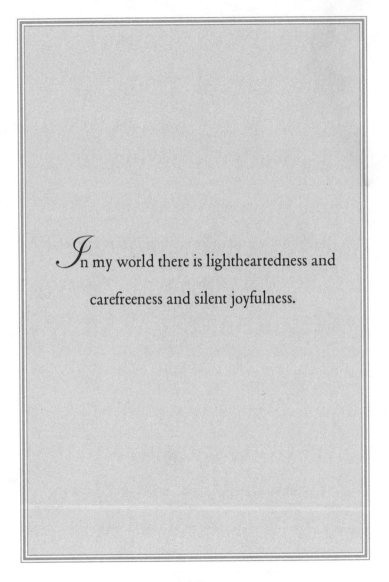

$\mathcal{I}$n my world there is lightheartedness and

carefreeness and silent joyfulness.

*I*n my world there is life in all its moods,

in all its contradictions, and in all its

manifestations.

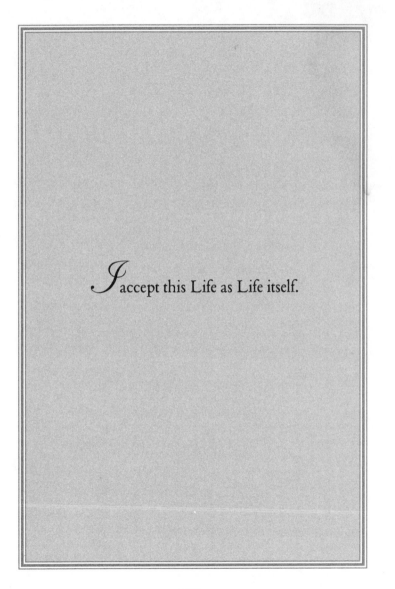

I accept this Life as Life itself.

*B*ecause I accept Life as Life,

in my world, nothing ever goes wrong.

In my Being is the Universe.

Personality is time bound. It comes about
when the present is identified with the past
and projected into the future.

Attention devoid of memory or anticipation is life-centered, present moment awareness. Life-centered, present moment, choiceless awareness is timeless.

*T*ime exists only as the continuity

of memory using the ego as an internal

reference point.

*M*y original state is always present

but not in manifestation.

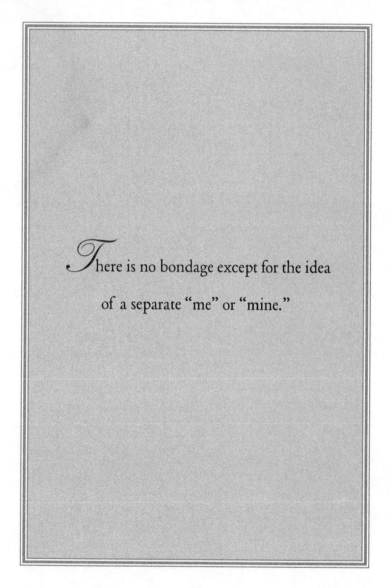

There is no bondage except for the idea

of a separate "me" or "mine."

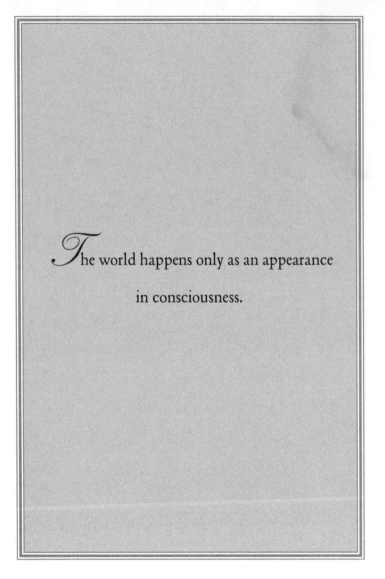

The world happens only as an appearance
in consciousness.

*T*he physical world of form and

phenomena is the totality of the known

manifested in the infinity of the unknown

unmanifest consciousness.

$\mathcal{I}$do nothing.

Being manifests, and living happens.

$\mathscr{I}$am that consciousness.

You are that consciousness.

All that exists is consciousness.

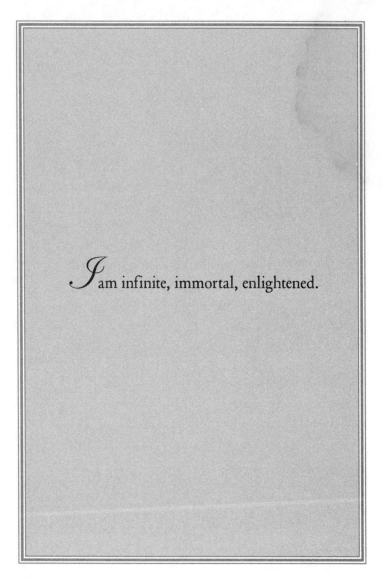

I am infinite, immortal, enlightened.

Infinity, immortality, enlightenment

are my natural state.

*M*y natural state is usually

overshadowed by the turbulence of the mind.

When I go past the dark alleys

and passages of my mind,

I come to the core of my Being.

*A*t the core of my Being I am in touch

with the light and the love and the

knowingness that are the inherent

properties of my natural state.

At the core of my Being is a principle,

an intelligence that generates, orchestrates

and organizes the activity of my mind

and of my body.

*W*hen I am in touch with the intelligence

(or principle) at the core of my Being and

I become intimate with it, I realize that this

same principle is at the core of all Beings

and orchestrates and organizes the mind and

body of all that lives and moves and breathes.

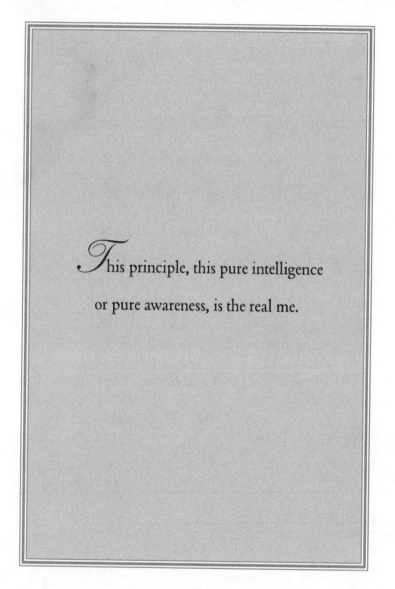

This principle, this pure intelligence

or pure awareness, is the real me.

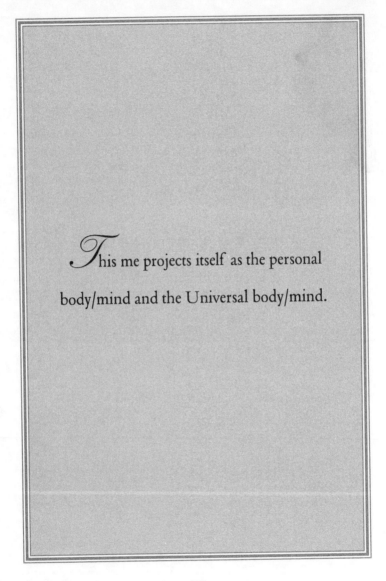

This me projects itself as the personal body/mind and the Universal body/mind.

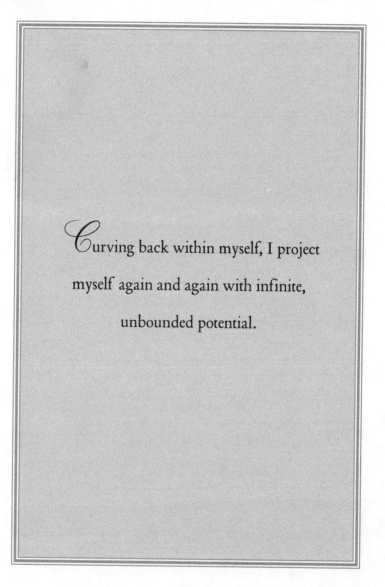

Curving back within myself, I project

myself again and again with infinite,

unbounded potential.

$\mathcal{I}$ am the animating force of life in all that

lives and moves and breathes in all Beings.

I am the light of love that is unity

consciousness.

I am the light of knowingness where

Creator, creating, and created are one.

At the deepest core of my Being is an
intelligence that is orchestrating the activity
of my mind and my body.

*W*hen I get in touch with the intelligence

at the deepest core of my Being, and become

intimate with it, I realize that the same

intelligence is orchestrating the activity of

other minds and other bodies—and, in fact,

all the activity in the Universe.

This intelligence at the deepest core of my

being, and of other Beings, and of the

Universe, has been called God by many

spiritual traditions.

At the deepest core of all Being is the

generator, organizer, and dispenser of all

the activity that exists in the Universe.

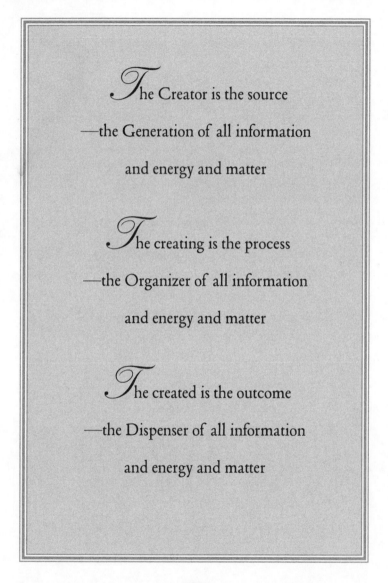

The Creator is the source

—the Generation of all information

and energy and matter

The creating is the process

—the Organizer of all information

and energy and matter

The created is the outcome

—the Dispenser of all information

and energy and matter

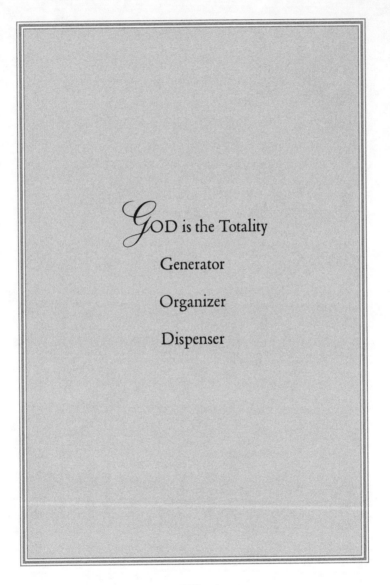

$\mathcal{G}$OD is the Totality

Generator

Organizer

Dispenser

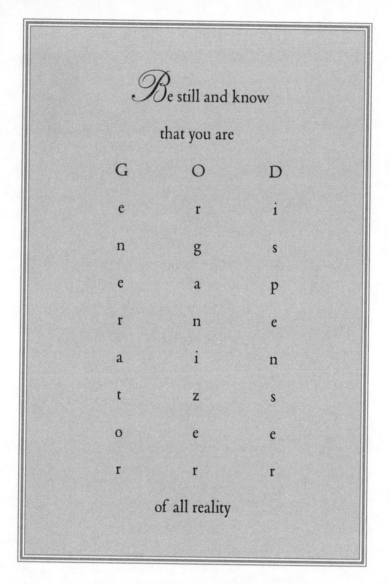

*B*e still and know

that you are

G	O	D
e	r	i
n	g	s
e	a	p
r	n	e
a	i	n
t	z	s
o	e	e
r	r	r

of all reality

CREATING AFFLUENCE
Wealth Consciousness in the Field of All Possibilities
A series of steps, each of which contains a seed of
knowledge that can be nourished in our daily lives
to achieve prosperity and abundance.
188٬003242٬2 New World Library hardcover

PERFECT WEIGHT
*The Complete Mind/Body Program for Achieving
and Maintaining Your Ideal Weight*
By becoming more aware of your Ayurvedic body type, you
can learn how to step outside often impossible cultural ideals
and enjoy the value in your own ideal weight and beauty.
0٬517٬88458٬5 Three Rivers Press softcover

RESTFUL SLEEP
The Complete Mind/Body Program for Overcoming Insomnia
Practical techniques for using the wisdom of Ayurveda
to soothe the senses, balance the physiology, and enjoy
the full restorative power of restful sleep.
0٬517٬88457٬7 Three Rivers Press softcover

JOURNEY INTO HEALING
Awakening the Wisdom Within You
Essential thoughts calibrated to create a shift in perception
and release the body's natural tendency to perfect health.
0٬609٬60498٬8 Harmony Books hardcover

THE SEVEN SPIRITUAL LAWS OF SUCCESS
A Practical Guide to the Fulfillment of Your Dreams
Timeless wisdom and practical steps distill the essence of
Dr. Chopra's teachings into seven simple yet powerful
principles that can easily be applied to create success
in all areas of your life.
1-878424-11-4   New World Library   hardcover

THE RETURN OF MERLIN
A novel that moves back and forth from the time of King
Arthur to present-day England, this rich tale is imbued with
the hope and transcendent power of spiritual awakening.
0-449-91074-1   Fawcett Books   softcover

BOUNDLESS ENERGY
The Complete Mind/Body Program
for Overcoming Chronic Fatigue
Practical steps for achieving balance—the key to living
life with energy, zest, and fulfillment.
0-609-80075-2   Three Rivers Press   softcover

PERFECT DIGESTION
The Key to Balanced Living
Strategies drawn from the Ayurvedic tradition address
the physical and emotional aspects of overcoming a wide
range of digestive ailments, from IBS to constipation.
0-609-80076-0   Three Rivers Press   softcover

THE WAY OF THE WIZARD
Twenty Spiritual Lessons for Creating the Life You Want
Spiritual alchemy to restore the magic in everyday life, drawing from
the wisdom of the great wizard Merlin of Arthurian legend.
0-517-70434-X   Harmony Books   hardcover

OVERCOMING ADDICTIONS
The Spiritual Solution
Working from the mind/body principle that addictions begin
by looking for the right thing in the wrong place, Dr. Chopra
proposes strategies for reintroducing the true experience of joy.
0-609-80195-3   Three Rivers Press   softcover

THE PATH TO LOVE
Spiritual Strategies for Healing
Timeless wisdom and practical advice combine to help clear
away obstacles and to restore the boundless miracle of love.
0-609-80135-X   Three Rivers Press   softcover

THE SEVEN SPIRITUAL LAWS OF PARENTS
Guiding Your Children to Success and Fulfillment
Dr. Chopra's answer to parents around the world wondering
how to raise their children with values that fulfill spiritual
needs as well as create the experience of abundance.
0-609-60077-X   Harmony Books   hardcover

RAID ON THE INARTICULATE
Poems by Deepak Chopra
Verses that celebrate life and spirit, salutations
to the nature of timeless reality.
1-882971-16-7   Infinite Possibilities Publishing   hardcover

THE LOVE POEMS OF RUMI
New translations of the Sufi poet whose writings reflect the deepest
longings of the human heart as it searches for the divine.
0/609/60243/8 Harmony Books hardcover

HEALING THE HEART
A Spiritual Approach to Reversing Coronary Artery Disease
Specifies suggestions for reducing risk factors by
following an individually tailored regimen
based on the principles of Ayurveda.
0/609/60035/4 Harmony Books hardcover

AGELESS BODY, TIMELESS MIND
The Quantum Alternative to Growing Old
Explores how applying the principles of mind/body medicine can
dramatically slow down and even reverse the aging process.
0/517/88212/4 Three Rivers Press softcover

PERFECT HEALTH
The Complete Mind/Body Guide
A practical guide to the science of Ayurveda,
a system of mind/body medicine that has its
roots in the ancient wisdom of India.
0/517/58421/2 Three Rivers Press softcover

About the Author

DEEPAK CHOPRA HAS WRITTEN TWENTY-THREE BOOKS, which have been translated into thirty-five languages. He is also the author of more than thirty audio and videotape series, including five critically acclaimed programs on public television. Chopra currently serves as the director for educational programs at The Chopra Center for Well Being in La Jolla, California.